Orchard Days

poems by

Heather Corbally Bryant

Finishing Line Press
Georgetown, Kentucky

Orchard Days

for my three children, with gratitude for our days of Eden

ACKNOWLEDGMENTS

"Gibbous Moon" previously published in *Practicing Yoga in a Former Shoe Factory* (Georgetown: Finishing Line Press, 2020)

"Apples" *Old Frog Pond Farm* poem of the month, October 2020

"Squam Lake" previously published in *Practicing Yoga in a Former Shoe Factory* (Georgetown: Finishing Line Press, 2020)

"Squannacook River" previously published in *Practicing Yoga in a Former Shoe Factory* (Georgetown: Finishing Line Press, 2020)

Publisher: Leah Huete de Maines
Editor: Christen Kincaid
Cover Art: Colin Page, *Apple Trees*
Author Photo: Richard Howard, www.richardhowardphotography.com
Cover Design: Elizabeth Maines McCleavy

Order online: www.finishinglinepress.com
also available on amazon.com

Author inquiries and mail orders:
Finishing Line Press
P. O. Box 1626
Georgetown, Kentucky 40324
U. S. A.

Table of Contents

The harvest is past, the summer has ended, and we are not saved.
—Jeremiah 8:20

Apples

Sometimes, they say, deer come at night to munch
Apples—we would pay our children pennies to pick
Up newly fallen ones—the ones without crunch marks—
We would mash these beauties into amber-colored
Cider; wasps would swarm on warm autumn days—
Sweetness trickling down from the red wheel of the
Machine we shared with our neighbor—we would fill
Our wheelbarrow with piles of crushed apples and
Take them to the woods where we toss them—they
Would lie there, undisturbed, until the stags would
Wander through our forest in herds, loping through
Dusk to pick up the leavings; still, the smell of apples
Recalls early twilight October Evenings—our years
There came very close, or so I thought, to days of Eden.

Orchard Days

In those days the mist rose early—we slept and
Slipped and woke—a buck stands by the garage door
When I take out the trash—when you are off,

Nowhere to be found—mist so thick the stag
Appears as a ghoul or phantom—have I imagined
Him? Conjured him up? So dense is the mist

Around me in our apple orchard, sweet smell
Of apples—crisp in November darkness, the
Line between the living and the dead—between

My imagining and my waking is slim indeed, so
Different do I will my world to be from how
It is—a stag, a buck, his horns come so close

They could touch—he stands still in the
Surrounding silence of descent.

At the Aquarium

The names read aloud delight—stingray, holocanthus, spotted wobbegong—
But the fish are the thing—as they swim through their underwater world—
Red bellied piranha flitter past spiny lobster, moon jelly shines, Blue Tang
Flame fish glitters, green moray eel slithers along the tank's bottom—

Next to the purple sea urchin, a horseshoe crab trawls for a new home among
The blue domus, white anemones, green glades of seagrass—

A whole alphabet is here, contained in this tiny universe far from the yellow drum
Aurelia Aurita to the black and white zebra dwarfish.

Our faces pressed close to the tank, supposedly invisible to the fish through the
One way glass, immersed in this silent, watery world—

We learn the safest place in a hurricane is among a mangrove swamp—always, in
These days, I am seeking safety, invisibility, a place where no one can shout at me,
Or touch me when I don't want to be touched—

But I don't know this then—memory consists of peeling back the layers, over
and again—

We keep company with the sergeant majors, and perhaps are lucky enough to stay
Out of the way of the iridescent and captivating blue poison dart frog—

Sea stars all, they draw me in—mesmerized by their motion, and the letters in their
Names—reciting the alphabet always stays me—whispering their names reassures
Me—Blacknose, Caranx hippos, Rock beauty—I cling to a magical belief that
knowing

What they are called will save me—but, all the knowledge in the world could
not save Eve.

Shark Tank, Sydney Aquarium

From below we watch, mesmerized
Through a glass tube—we look up and
Around at sharks swimming hungry
Past us, circling back again with sharp
Teeth bared—

We learn an adult fish replaces its
Weapon at the average rate of one
Set a week—hence the ivory is never
Dull—

But precious when we find it on the
Beach—look, a shark's tooth, we cry
Out, slipping the soft worn piece in

Our pocket.

Carousel, Chicago

In late afternoon July
Painted horses take us
By surprise, beside the

Aquamarine tinted lake,
A lone man sits ready to
Turn the crank, play music,

Make animals dance—a
Ride just for the two of us,
You, my daughter, face

Upturned in joy against
The wind, warmed by sun,
Smiling with the pleasure

Of unexpected frivolity.

Three Pelicans

Against an azure sky three
Black pelicans swoop across
Puffy clouds, searching for

Tasty fish; they fly free, true,
Gliding low together, intent
On their task, a trio, triad,

Triplets, triplicate, swirling
Low on a windless day—one,
Two, three, they dive, breaking

Ocean's surface, making wakes,
Swept high on a wave's crest
Where foam froths as each

Bird takes off, silver dinner
Pressed in beaks, not one
Backward glance to shore.

Surf

Turquoise wall of water
Poised to turn, roll over
Itself, rippling along, end
To end—

In the instants before white
Foam froths, a clear view
Emerges through—a

Glimpse of the shelter I
Seek before sand roils up,

Churning this miniature
Ecosystem—shells and rocks

Come crashing to shore,
Rushing inland with salty

Tide, salt stings all wounds
Before they can be healed.

Water Moccasins

We come around a bend where three men are
Circling a shining mass swirling and writhing

On hot pavement—one man wields a big stick,
Another drags over a hunting dog, one more is

Poised behind a wheel ready to gun his engine,
To kill, destroy, smother the reptile in all its

Blackness—a young boy comes running from
A nearby house, carrying a wooden timber

Bigger than he is—he begins to beat the snake—
Motion quickens, coils proliferate, slinking across

The road, seeking earth, water, far away from

The massacre—

I look away—and ask my children to do the same—

We drive around the battleground.

Much later that night, as I sneak into bed alone,
Before he can get there—I understand what we have seen—

 A mother snake guarding her young against human cruelty.

Kayaking by Kinnakeet

Bright sun, small ripples of wind—paddles gliding across
The sound, past a bevy of orange-footed ducks, four snowy

White egrets—around a tiny island until we land on a beach
Beside a grassy inlet—we pull our vessels to shore so as to

Explore a grove of old shade trees, gnarled, gray, hunched

From years of westward blowing storms—here on this island

In a village which takes its name from a river in England, here
An Algonquin word meaning that which is mixed—

Amidst stubby mounds of grass, we see six white marble

Gravestones mostly hidden among tufts of greenery—we

Make out lines of remembrance, tracing letters with our fingers—

A family of Williams, who died just over a century ago—here on
This small island, in a new world I am learning is a prison to me.

Electric Air

Black August clouds loom southeastward piling high, one atop
Another, circling horizon's edge—air is sticky, heavy, low-pressure,

Barometer falling—flies begin to bite, taking angry nips on my
Ankles—we jump water and wave—as we make our way towards

Shore we hear thunder's first clap—a pod of dolphins jump,
Dorsal fins leaping above churning water—there is stillness before

A bolt of lightning cracks the sky open—we should dash for home,

Toes tingling from the ions of electricity flashing along sand—
Our world has been plugged into a giant socket—

We should not be anywhere close to this electricity storm—

We might as well be plugging our wet fingers into charged outlets.

Lives of a Shell

"Can I come too?"
My daughter asks—

Together, we walk over boardwalk,
Down steps sifted with sand, to
Where water laps the land—

So simple. Earth, water, air-
By habit, or inclination, she seeks
Miniature clams hiding under
Holes until she has collected

Two handfuls; we make a haiku—

Brown feet squelch heavy and,
We head to a higher, dry spot

On the beach—usually, I walk
This stretch alone, but now I
Have company—

Here is my hope for you—
I whisper a silent wish in this
Place where I first heard these

Magical words on the phone
With a genetics specialist at

A hospital in Boston:
"Congratulations. You're going
To have a daughter, 46xx."

Carolina Moon

When you stand outside your life for an instant, you
Might be able to see something as if for the first time—

Curving roads, stony walls, green apple trees leafing over
Into crisp newness of autumn—and then, in memory,

You shut your eyes, waiting for dusk, on the sand swept
Barrier islands where you finally see everything—

What you once thought was yours, all of it—is not—

You thought you were the snail carrying your life's
Belongings on your back—you return to the fragments

To realize that, when you were not looking, everything
Has slipped away from you, has slipped off your back

And been taken away, mostly not by you—all that was

Precious, true,

Is gone—

Against a sky stretched out full and clear, an orange disk
Of a crescent moon is rising, eclipsing the orb's shadows—

Leaving behind what was once made, and then remade in hope
And in blind trust—

Looking at the sliver of what remains behind you realize that, once
You leave, you can never again return to this place.

The most dangerous time for a woman is the time when her
Abuser realizes she might leave; the second most dangerous

Time is the first three months after she leaves for the first time.

Brush Clearing

You set a fire to the winter brush we've cleared—leftover
Pruning from our apple trees—splinters, sticks, and limbs—

Down at the end of our garden where we grew frail pumpkins,
You pour gasoline over the debris and strike a match—

The fire blares all day in anger and in desperation—you stand
There, fury smoldering, as it often did with you—

You who feels the world has left you behind, has not been kind to you—

I stay away, having learned early that your moods are dangerous,
Your fire can flare way too quickly—whatever I do or say will

Not be what you want, will be held against me—it is dusk before
The embers darken—the fire chief has come by twice to

Issue a warning, a fact which remains unbeknownst to me.

Almost

For dwj

They rushed you away moments after your early arrival
In that bright white hospital delivery room—I knew

Something had gone wrong—but I had another baby to
Birth, afterpains to ride through, a ruptured placenta and a

Hemorrhage to endure—hours later, in darkness, I caught
First sight of you—splayed on your tiny bed, spread out like

A miniature eagle captured on a table—splints on your wrists
With miniscule needles stuck in your thimble-like arms,
An IV in your head, your blue knitted cap pushed to the side—

I wanted you swaddled, cuddled like a newborn—not displayed
Like a medical specimen—through my medicine-laced eyes I

Catalogued what I could see: leafy green ferns hanging from the ceiling,
Nurses with polished red nails clicking around, checking tubes,

Writing on charts—I couldn't yet hold your fish body that night,
But if I promised to rest maybe I would be lucky the next.

My Daughter in Third Grade

for pej

Just running off the bus,
You look up at me with
Wisdom—blue eyes

Stare through glasses—
Wise, like an owl—

At that instant, you
Laugh, a rich giggle,
Amused by your own

Thoughts. As if you
Yourself can be
Contained in a universe

Filled with words, full
And true, turned
Sidewise, a world all

Your own, belonging
All to you, not to any
One else.

To the Edge of the Light

We drive through harsh rains, slippery pavements, rows
And rows of sputtering trucks, spots of diesel smoke cloud

The view of green hills rolling, tumbling away from us—

I tense against time and ride—somewhere in the middle
Of New York, past dairy cows standing by red barns, doors

Open for the night, a whiteness glows across the skies—

Sunset spreads new, like in a painting illuminating a dusky
Museum wall somewhere in a small town in France—

We are in the middle of nowhere and yet, we are everywhere—

Your mood has been stormy, glum, impatient—I

Cannot allow myself to fear what I know is to come

When we arrive where we are going.

The Line Turned Blue

for wbj

Long before the line turned blue, I began to imagine you—
Conceived in a March with two moons—first I was sleepy,

Then sick, by turns excited and terrified—your cells multiplied
Inside me faster than I could imagine—

I first saw your face in June—you were lying crosswise, floating
In fluid, sleeping—still, I wouldn't feel you much, just a little

Flip now and then—you were quiet, sleepy—just as you were
That Sunday December morning—it was dark when I went into

Labor with you—and it was dark again by the time you were
Born—

The nurse called you a sleepy boy, then I knew you were you—

You turned blue when they put you on my chest for the first
Time—they pounded on your heels until you breathed again—

Your first night on earth you cried, filled with the terror and
Wonderment of being alive—I held you and we two fell

Asleep until pink dawn began to rise in Boston over the slice of
The Toronto-Dominion garden I could see from my room.

Amber Alert

A child, two children have gone missing on an Indiana afternoon in July—
Their mother reports they have not turned up after visiting their father—

My son comes to me afraid—he has heard a crackled warning blasting
Over the pool's loudspeaker—he has listened to all the details—

I explain this is an unlikely event, though what I do not say is that it is
Far too common for my liking, a fact I find terrifying.

Sunflowers Outside Elmira

i.

It's always gray on this stretch of road, scattered showers
Threaten, maybe thunder later—clouds fill sky, casting

Opaque light over trees and rivers—there are no shadows,
Every last thing appears of equal weight, one thing and

Then the other—rows of corn, grass, and wheat scatter on—

As far as I can see—there is only green and more of it.

ii.

Sunflowers turn to face the sun, wherever it may be, follow its
Progression throughout the day long—a whole field of

Bright yellow and orange flowers dotted with black-
Tipping centers—each turn towards the other—a whole

Field waiting, green stalks quivering.

iii.

Jesus is Coming, someone has scrawled in blue ink outside
A roadside bathroom stall—the human condition is, of

Necessity, based on hope; otherwise, why would we be
Here—

iv.

Sometimes knowledge requires more than hope to survive,
Wisdom is required to stay alive—

v.

Sunflowers turn towards sunshine, a whole field whispers.

Najaf

These places exist only on maps in my head—
Terrain unknown, somewhere far away where

Soldiers go—sometimes I see a cargo plane
Taking off early in the morning, flying over

Our pond, the pond where my children swim—
Just before the blue heron makes its rounds—

A khaki desert vehicle will sometimes zoom down
The highway whose hum we can hear at night—

A woman in battle fatigue will come into the
General store for a drink, carrying her lunch in a

Brown paper bag—I turn down the front page of a
Newspaper so that my children won't see photos of the

Latest bombing over Iraq—the insurgents battle
Again—for the umpteenth time, more than I

Can count, I wonder why we went to war after all—
And those who will bear the cost, who should not.

To Czeslaw Milosz

"How do you write about suffering and still be able to approve of the world at the same time?"
—CM

You died yesterday—seems impossible that you would succumb like any
Other mortal—

Just recently, your words comforted me—the image of a worn stone church
In a mountain village—green grass, fields, warm wild strawberries—

Sweetness after long rains, your words make sense to me in the midst of
Ineffable tragedy—you could let me see anew there would be a fresh

Day to live, a poem to write, a walk to take—

I know I'm going to miss you.

Things That Fall From the Sky

How to explain to the children
Things that fall from the sky—
Airplanes that are steered, reckless,
Hapless into buildings, pilots hit on the head,
Skyscrapers toppling on a glorious September
Morning—

Other carriers almost saved, flown into a field
To burn—and not so long after, a space shuttle
Blown to smithereens in the atmosphere—

Particles falling across America—yes, these
Things happen, rarely, but they do—
I cannot say otherwise.

Planting Pansies

I planted pansies in pots today, fluttering
Stems, brittle against new gusts—soil
Damp, untouched—spade by spade I
Plodded ahead—when I looked up, all
Blooms were opening—bright spots of
Vermillion centered in creamy whiteness—
Sapphire blue, velvet midnight—black
Creases in centers—

By dusk, the temperature had dropped
Almost forty degrees, and by bedtime,
The mercury stood well below freezing—
Luckily, pansies are of hearty stock, I'm
Told they can survive a first frost with ease.

The Thickening

At first, in a darkened room, a doctor waved her wand over
My swollen belly—there's a head, a foot, a thumb—over there,
Is the second one, sleeping at the moment, behind her twin—
It's too difficult to check the face for abnormalities, too difficult
To see—there, she paused and clicked her instruments to take
A measurement; she said nothing—only later in the hallway, I
Thought she gave me a strange look, a second glance—it was
Only later, in another doctor's office that I learned of her
Concern; the neck on one twin had thickened, correlating with
Certain birth abnormalities; I cried all the way home—it was
August, the light thickening, traffic humming, cicadas chirping—
As night fell, I could feel the humbling of being a parent beginning.

Gibbous Moon

Round white paper lantern hanging
Behind a trail of pink clouds like
Feathers spread out from a pillow—
As twilight comes, the clouds pass—
Turning to lavender cream until
They've fled stage right.

Moon rises high, and fast—
By supper's end, twilight has
Fallen, crepuscular—and then,
Not a speck of down remains,
Just one big satellite presides,
Phoebus in a gibbous phase.

To a Daughter, Age Nine

When I see your nine-year-old self look,
Owl-like, back at me—wise in your blue
Glasses, studs of azure eyes returning
My gaze, I think of the many words I could
Say to you, but something stops me stark
And fast—it is you, I think, who will have

Answers for me—that is, if I can listen for
Whatever it is you might want to tell me—

What I might be lucky enough to hear—
Ever since I learned I was expecting you—
46xx—I have been waiting for you to
Emerge—from the get-go you have had a
Sure and free self, formed in full wherever
Else you were before you came here.

White Fox

One shadow crosses a farmer's field—
Lush grass in late afternoon sun—all
We see is a flash of silver; when we stop
The creature halts too, becoming a
Statue shining against the land's
Dullness—

As long as we are still, so he remains
Frozen, caught in suspended motion—
When we move on, he waits as if
To assure we are for real before he
Runs off into a pine-green forest—

As he disappears into the oncoming
Darkness, I realize he is limping,
Dragging one leg behind, tail flashing
Light—

Above, a full halo moon is rising,
Silver against phosphorescent blue
Of the falling night—

Old Mill Pond Path

Through wet oak leaves we stomped,
Rain pattering heavier and heavier—
Until our hair was soaked, pressed
Close to our heads, we tromped along
A ridge, then up a steep hill, climbing
Hard and close to the sky, passed rocks
Covered with soft and spiny lichen in
Various shades of green, leprechaun
Forest, mushrooms sprouting in damp,
Acorn pairs, empty, having fallen
From the trees, scattering our way—

Until we came to the place where
Boulders had sliced the land in two in
Some long ago edge, leaving a deep
Crevice which we could not cross, where
A gentle farmer had once tried to stem
The course of a stream rushing down to
A round pond—moving the harsh boulders
He'd taken and pried up from the fields
Where he had once hoped to plant.

Where I Come From

i.

Still water, rainbow light one red
Chrysanthemum stuck in a glass jar
Reflecting all that lies around—sun,
Moon, earth, stars, grass, soot—
Blackbirds and Mars—

ii.

Of this I am sure: I do not come
From where I once thought.

iii.

Drops of semen were warm,
Fresh, but they did not belong
To my father—instead, a doctor
Loaned his own, mixed them, as
They called it then—until the strands
Of DNA wound together, piercing
One egg from my mother.

iv.

No one would be the wiser, not
Then, not ever, or so they thought,
But for a slip of the tongue, a
Universe toppled, set slant on its
Side, paternity recalled, reclaimed.

A Hummingbird

Like a humming bird whirring, diving, I fly to nectar—
Spying it from afar—my body jiggles, wiggles, bumps
Along the way, through darkness and disarray—until
I am turning in circles upon myself—

Forcing my wings through brambles, nettles, burrs
Threatening to pull me to the ground—disrupting
My flight with all their might—

When I land beside a sweet bowl of liquid, put out by
Some kind soul, I sip until the loveliness fills my beak—
Wondering up at sky blue skies until there can be no
Possible retreat—

Until I can soar high as can be, evening my speed so I
Can balance my wings on pretended truth.

Early Snow

Overnight, frost turned the world white—from
Hedgerow over stone wall stretching to field
Beyond—each leaf, bough, and stone etched

In clear crystals, see through, translucent, there
For all light to catch—as sun began to shine,

Quiet came with stealth, silence too—as we
Woke up to see what had happened here—
How flakes had come, piling on themselves,

Fluffier and fluffier, until all color had vanished—
Been replaced by monochromatic spectrum—

A blanket covering our earth, here til springtime—
As we ourselves draw in to our centers, put
Dried logs on our hearths, strike matches, we

Lament early darkness, longing for the past
Summer days, snow a reluctant reminder
Recalling to our minds wintry beauty.

New Year's Day

We take such stock in calendars,
Turning over a blank page, as if
There could be something
So clear as a fresh start;
Teasing ourselves, we set
Rules, regulations, tabulations
About when and where
We need to be.

Taming the great unknown,
The open spaces of our lives,
We divide our days into hours,
Then into minutes, seconds,
Instants, appointing meeting
Dates, rendezvous, illicit or
Otherwise; we try to keep our
Word, but all the same

We hesitate when events
Hem us in, all of a sudden our
Months fill and we stare down
Writing not our own not of our
Own choosing, until we begin
To see the first step towards
Being free is to start with our heart.

The Red Planet

Even at this late hour, we
Seek to know what we cannot,
To go where we might have
Been barred; thousands of
Miles away, a little metal
Rover lands on a planet,
Scampers round, beams
Images of a craggy landscape
Touched with red, and blue too—
Unfolding along the horizon.

Back on earth, we don glasses,
And peer up at a sky full still
Of wonder and mystery to
Think there might be a chance
We could see inside the universe's
Secrets, that the globe strung up
In classrooms everywhere, the
Sphere that is Mars could
Somehow be ours.

Feast of Three Kings

Clear light, open views—
Sun hangs low in the sky,
We seek evening hues,
As a moonrise comes
High over twilight.

A rush of blue air
Turns to black, then
Back again to white
As we wait for night,
For purity of vision

Which comes only on
This early evening of a
New Year; we trick
Ourselves into seeing
Where all rivers start—
Just there, in the heart.

Downside Up, Oceania

Here is the farthest I've ever been—
Thousands upon thousands of
Miles away from where I call home—

South of the equator—into another
Day, several time zones away—

Everything is different—stars, light,
Night, swirls of water go the
Other way—in the morning,

I look out at bright mountain ranges
In full summer—upside down, right side
Up—it's a whole new world

Where expeditions for the Antarctic
Depart from the tarmac—a whole
New way of being comes to me

As we cross the Tasman Sea.

Southern Cross

In the fullness of dark now, not a light to be
Found anywhere—we drive on through the
Night—

Through mountain passes separating the
Remarkables, fields, down to clear cut
Streams running through rocks, flecks of

Water flashing, lit by stars—

I peer up through pillowy black—a whole
Array of constellations begins to blink on—

Not a familiar one there—I remember to
Look for the Southern Cross, the sky is

Different here, in this hemisphere.

The Last Day of February

If divinity lies within us,
Then we may take a pass
At grace—fill our lives

With the hope of redemption—
That when we take our leave,
We will know we have

Accomplished something—
At least one thing of beauty—

That we have come and
Witnessed, borne children,

Laughed, and shared in the simple,
Yet singular faith of the everyday.

Lilacs

Early May, lilacs come through, hard buds
New and purple, softening in the sun, a huge
Bush of them sprinkles color and beauty
Down the whole city block—

There, just for the asking, outside the fence—
A woman waits for the bus, red scarf pulled
Up against her neck against the chill—

No one is looking, she peers around, glancing
To see if anyone might see her—she is
Apparently alone on the street—

With surreption she reaches her hand
Up through the greenery, wrapping her fingers
Around a wad of purple blooms, pulling as
Hard as she can—

Until a branch has broken off; she clasps it
In her left hand, safe as she waits—

Partings

The remarkableness of any us ever being able to let go—
I see you—being whisked away, oxygen mask over your
Face, just before the anesthesia has kicked in—
You, at the top of a ski slope in a snowstorm—your
Face clenched in annoyance at the bus stop—you
Don't want to go to school today, nor do you want to
Stay home—

Each morning, a slip knot of trust knits itself as you go—
And you return—each of us returns changed, if only
Slightly—wiser, perhaps, always in the process of
Beginning and of letting be—

This Plane is Being Taken out of Service

How little any of us understands—
We see turbulence rock around us—
We hear tales of torture, maiming,
Beheading, knives brandishing—in
That moment between not knowing
And knowing, the informing—

All else slips away; how much we
Have to trust every single day—
A summer's noontime—all three
Children in a row on an airplane—
Below fire engines circle the tarmac—
Ten minutes after take-off we hear,
This plane will be landing soon—

"Hold those kids tight," the man
Behind me leans forward to say—
I watch you—my children each
Absorbed in coloring a page of your
Own design—I cinch your seat belts
As small as they will go—

The plane's nose dips down, wheels
Touch landing strip—we taxi to a gate—
"This plane is being taken out of
Service," is all the captain says—
My son leans towards the window,
"Mommy, there's a lot of fire engines—"

My stomach knots, the crew waves us
Towards the lighted red exit sign—
Passengers gather suitcases, hats,
Windbreakers—no one speaks as we
Walk back into the terminal—

Between a setting out and an arriving,
So many missteps can occur—

The wonder is, we close our minds,
Move on, never stopping to ask what
We are doing here—
A long line forms to rebook our
Tickets on the next plane to Chicago—

Fight

I hear a visceral scream coming from the front porch—an
Animal in pain—children cry for help—the black dog has our
Gray cat in her mouth, teeth all over her belly—the feline
Writhes in pain, scratching back, harder this time—

You jump in and pull the dog's collar, the cat digs her claws—
Two creatures locked in a grimace of torture, neither one of
Them can bear to give the other up until you startle them into
Letting go—

The cat slinks away, licking her wounds—we drag the dog inside—
She shakes off her disgrace, collar jingling—

I pull one cat claw out of nose; she stands still—only decades later,
Will I see this scene as a metaphor buried inside my life.

Pasture

Every day, I pass this field—green grass stretches across a meadow,
Ringed by weathered gates, an old stone fence—here before any one of
Us—every day, I see this mother and daughter, and mare and her calf—
A year ago, they were nuzzling, the young one still unsteady on her feet—
Now each stands beside to the other, silent, passing their days together
Without any other expectation than what the presence of love can provide.

Squam Lake

It is so simple, now I see, you cannot own me,
Nor could you ever—you still assume it's like
That awful day in June when I came home from
A lake with a man not my husband and you
Turned your back on me, refusing to look at or
Speak to me for many days—now I see that was
Not your right, not your provenance—you couldn't
Claim me, not then, not now, not ever—no
Human being can ever claim ownership over
Another—how different a history of the world
Would be if no one ever owned anyone else—
Not as slave, whore, mother, lover, husband, child—
We each belong to ourselves, a lesson it has
Taken me most of a lifetime to learn.

This Dream I've Had

I've only had one recurring dream in my life—every night
It was the same—I was not really married to my first husband—
Something always stood in the path of an official marriage—
Whenever the dream came, it would be enough to remind
Me of some unfinished work which remained to be done—

I would awaken startled, surprised, unsure, yet every day I
Would turn away from what my dream might have been
Warning me of—something in my life was not right—I buried
The problem so deep in my psyche I would be sure not to find it—
Buried far beneath the earth—until my husband told me I

Was going crazy—that was when I knew I had to leave him.
Once he had left the house, that particular nightmare was gone.

Embryos

It was hot that day in June;
On the drive to Boston, skyscrapers
Sliced through humid gray air.
By the time we'd arrived, sun
Had broken through thick clouds.
When they wheeled me into the
Operating room, giddiness floated
Above me—let's go for as many
As we can—pretty soon, five
Glistening embryos had been
Inserted deep inside me—but
Not before I'd glimpsed these
Miracles swirling in test tubes—

As days passed, I grew more
Skeptical, unabashed, unsure until
I had talked myself into the idea
That it hadn't worked, for sure—
Already I had seen some blood—
So convinced I was that I cried for
All the sorrows of the world, lives
Lost, chanced missed—until my
Body told me otherwise; I felt
Different. Congratulations, the
Doctor said in the message on
My answering machine:
 You are very pregnant.

Secrets

I grew up with secrets—learning that big and little were all mixed up—
The sperm was warm, my mother said, but we don't know for sure whose it
Was—honey, we can explain everything—yes, your father was married
Before, ten years long, no children, his wife left him for another man
Instead, a marriage like a funeral, the bride wore navy blue, she was in
Mourning for what had already been—to get to that moment where they
Promised each to the other but then there was that doubt, that sense of
What had not been, could not be, shredding the hope out of a series of
Promises broken, instead of understanding what had grown quietly, when
No one was looking, like green ferns coming up among trees in the dark
Forest where long shadows are cast deep in the soft pillows of pine needles.

What I Would Give You

for my children

We talk about the towers and how they came topping down,
Buildings no one ever thought could fall; they were the tallest
In the world until then—it is impossible to explain how absurd
This world has become, how these people planned to disturb
The universe on a bright fall morning, chosen because it had
No clouds—in its aftermath, we worry about what might have
Been, or what could have come to pass—we only have each day,
This day, to call our own—in the meantime, I would give you
Forgiveness and peace in your soul, the ability to amuse yourself
Under all conditions, to make other plans when necessary, to
Keep yourself afloat in the water, warm for a night in the woods;
Most of all, how to keep yourself passionate about something,
Whatever it may be, that whatever else, the desire must come
From inside your own hearts—in the meantime, you will know
What that is only when you happen upon it—it will consume you
And keep you alive, not otherwise; only then will you
Know what you have come here to do.

Letter from Baghdad

It is hot here, damnable so—
Sand stirs and stings our faces, day after day,
We go round, house by house, looking for
Infidels, ingrates, renegades, anyone who
Might toss a bomb into a crowded street,
Behind a truck, the orders come down
Differently, every now and then a sergeant
Changes his mind, tells us to interrogate
Someone, torture them, hang them up
Somewhere, near or far, they don't care.
At home, no one even cares there's a war on—

It's not called a war anymore, simply keeping
The peace, the peace we tried to break, then
Make, then say it wasn't so—here there are
Tanks, guerillas, the threat of dirty bombs
Hidden away somewhere, no one can say—
How or why things became the way they are—
It's just what isn't so—here I sit and remember
Life in my small town at home, the green
Common, the brick library, most of all the blue
Floating water, ebbing across the beach at dusk.

Tigris River

These marines sent so far away cast a body
Into the water—what can one person do—too
Few to be able to know—stories, we hear, terrible
Ones too—and we wonder half a world away, there
Is not much left to say; we come up short, the ugly
American takes on a whole new meaning; if all of us
Continue down the same road, not one of us will be able
To own up to it—not that we would want to anyway.

Waiting

In a time years ago which now seems farther
Away than I can fathom—we waited for you
To be born—it is a time I cannot describe when
Loss seemed to reside inside—mostly monthly—
Your almost eleven-year-old wisdom now looks
Up at me, "You mean, you had three babies who
Died inside your tummy—?" Well, "yes and no,
Perhaps not exactly," I begin, "It was early, you
See, and there was probably something wrong—"
I thought I would never forget an instant of
Those days, but I was incorrect, you see—you
Now push life through me—the ghosts fade.

Morning on Longwood Avenue

The news came upon me slowly that wintry morning—
You had both been born, and had survived your first
Snowy night—the first forty-eight hours would be
The riskiest, so the doctors said; nurses came to
Check on me, my blood count, my enduring headache,
My private wounds—giving birth had not been easy—
"Those twins gave you a tough time," the resident
Remarked—I nodded, but inside I said, oh, how I
Wanted them—while my nurse was looking the
Other way, I snuck around, gripping my bed so I
Could partially stand—"what are you doing up and
Around?"—"I'm going to see my babies,"—not now,
She said, repeating, "not now" holding a packet of
Smelling salts under my nose—you are most certainly
Not going alone, and you must wait for your
Wheelchair to arrive—and for me to be free again.

Winter Orchard

In late afternoon haze, almost dusk—a herd
Of deer graze on fallen apples lying underneath
The snow, newly-fallen; if we listen closely, we
Can almost hear them crunch; they shimmer
In the distance, their bodies folding into the
Mirage that becomes twilight—I wonder how
They are related, one to the other, and
Whether they live on this hill, roaming from
One orchard to the next; there is no stag
With them tonight—perhaps only two fawns
Standing alone, their mothers just close by.

Gaza Girl

You stand in line, waiting to return to school with
Your friends, afternoon lessons just scheduled
To begin when a shot comes out of the blue to kill
You—nowhere here is safe, only an endless storm
Of fire from one to the other—as though your life
Was only waiting to begin again; what has been
Said before remains to torture, the remains of
What cannot be saved or blessed or understood,
But must vanish, as countries argue over borders,
Over who may own what, over what cannot be
Named, the circles of possession, grave promises
Broken, just as soon forgotten.

Paternity Songs

I learn so many lessons: how to hold a teacup,
Finger curved around the slim handle, how to use
A grapefruit soon to cut the membranes into neat
Segments, how to respond to a formal wedding
Invitation—the words repeat, I register these
Instructions; I memorize these rules of infinitesimal
Order—but then in the same breath, you tell me
Matters of so much more difficulty, matters far
Beyond the usual rules of life—on a dappled
Spring day in our orchard, you tell me we are
Not sure my father is my father, at least, we're not
Entirely sure, the sperm was mixed at the start,
To help the others along, to keep your father's strong—
And by the time you tell me, he's gone, so I cannot ask
Him for the truth, as I did on so many other occasions.

Birth, Petri Dish

A person consists of what—of air, water, blood, and soul—
All in the mix together, these parts begin in a heart
Pumping, lungs pushing air, a cluster of cells, a
Blastocyte begins to make a being, growing quickly,
Duplicating, replicating strands slipping over one another
Many times—a silver line of water until a circle is formed,
To become attached, to make new, to grow until a baby is born—
How little we make of this miracle consisting of name,
Date, weight and time—only the recorded facts
When our words fail in contemplation of the eternal
Mystery of the origins of life—when I see the embryologist
After my pregnancy has been confirmed, she stops to
Tell me that the two four-cell embryos that have taken
Were among the most beautiful she'd ever seen.

A Witch

Once I hated you, found you evil, tempting, plucking the silver
Apples from our trees—did you know it's bad luck not to leave
A few apples on the ground after harvest for the Faerie Folk—it
Is, after all, the fruit of the Otherworld—you took the apples from
Our trees before we could have our own private feast—I tried to
Banish you from our kingdom, told you to stay away but such
Was not to be—nolo tangere did not make sense to you—you
Were dangerous—hot to the touch—did you know it's even worse
Luck to cut down or destroy an apple tree—the unlawful cutting
Of an apple tree was formerly punishable by death under an
Ancient Brehon law—even though you pretended, you did not
Listen to a word I said—I believe you knew exactly what you were
Doing—you were responsible for providing the temptation—
And now I know you would never stop breaking your promises—
In this war I could not win, all I could do was leave our orchard.

Eccyesis

i.
In those days it was all about beginnings—trying to make them,
Making them, and then losing them all over again—one Sunday
Morning in early March I lost the start of a child—the baby slipped
Away, first stuck, then removed forcibly from my body—the hope of a
Life too young to know, only cells glistening in a dish, starting to
Go the wrong way, to grow outside my uterus—I remember the
Sorrow, the pain, the startling, the dream I had to hold on to—

ii.
My pain baffled the doctors—by all rights it should be gone,
It was not—yet then again, every test showed I was not pregnant—
But somewhere inside my body an embryo was growing—the search
Was on to find it—I learned new words like: extra-uterine, tubal,
Metacyesis—not the sort of words I had known co-existed with
Pregnancy—on the saddest day of my surgery I learned about the
Excruciating process of removing a pregnancy, the body does not

iii.
Make it easy—the blastocyte had strayed, so it would be more
Accurate to say I lost a pregnancy that was already lost far
Inside me—for weeks afterwards, I had to return to the hospital
For blood tests to make sure my numbers were dropping, the
Only proof the pregnancy was over had dissolved—
And I had to be told these results
Over and again from my extremely pregnant doctor.

Two Moons

In the middle of that long March, I must have ovulated twice,
My body yearning and leaning towards making a life, loathe to
Let go of the idea of creating, nourishing, birthing a life—

You came out of a night of astrological mystery, a March with
Two moons—in promise of the days to come, a pact with the
Universe, a result of the unearthly hope of better days to come—

And the idea of you kept me alive—as I watched you grow
Inside me, nestled in comfort, hope, and serenity—you showed
Me how life could be lived—in innocence, clarity, and beauty.

I protected you, the best I could, from the darkness spreading
From just past our orchard, the shadows emanating from the
Circling forest, the harbinger of foxes, hares, skunks, fisher cats, animals

Of extreme bestiality, creatures seeking only to satisfy their own desires.

Squannacook River

Here river swirls, eddies pushed right past us; we set out
With anticipation born of any human experience: preparation,
Explanation, launch—you sit at the head of the canoe, my
Paddling partner—almost too cool now to be seen with me—
But you are distracted by what we see: red-winged black
Birds, a pair of Baltimore Orioles, beaver scent mounds, to
Establish territory as well as to attract mates; best of all, we
Spot a Great Blue Heron flying over us all—

In a moment of silence, all is calm—we close our eyes, listen
To sounds of water, bird, faraway bulldozer, frog—on the way
Back, we pass seven painted turtles splayed on a sun-tipped
Rock—

On the return, we have wind at our backs; it is easy to see
Why we have come.

Mercury

i.

After a bitter, brutal winter the temperature
Begins to climb, ground thaws, we see small
Signs spring will come, again—

ii.

Not taking that for granted, I don't know
Any more, I have learned it remains a mystery
For me, to believe that spring will follow

iii.

Winter all over again—it is an act of faith
To believe in the divinity of the seasons—
In morning time, I see twigs beginning to

iv.

Bud brown, I hear a Phoebe bird sing, I know
I will carry with me the show of one male
Cardinal still fluttering about the apple

v.

Trees—we have to watch the mercury
Closely—too warm a March could signal
Disease, a harming of the silver apples

vi.

Softened in snow, the ones still germinating
In our trees, undisturbed by jealousy,
Rage, the hurling words of spite and

vii.

Hate, the belittling of Eve, the woman who
Was wronged right from the start.

The First of March

On the first of March, we drove
You home—six pounds tucked into
Layers of thick blankets—blue eyes,
Shut tight, black curly hair matted under
Your yellow knit cap—the one I wanted to
Keep for your baby, but which
Somehow disappeared in the haze
Of those early days—

We carried you out of the car,
Over the threshold of our new
House—I lay your still sleeping
Self right next to your twin brother
Who was wriggling, wiggling,
Cooing—waiting for you.

Orchards Burning

A puff of smoke crosses the sky,
Walking by we see new green coming
Now—rows of stubs, trees cut down,
Apple wood piles high—

Blue skies stretch tight—the road turns,
We linger, looking at the bonfire
Gathering steam, flames shooting
Out with wildness—

A change is bound to come, but
Maybe it can be slow, not too
Jarring; so far, this town has held
Off a lot, but there's always

A builder lurking, threatening to
Make clusters of houses dot the land,
Drawing families to set down their
Roots among the dwindling
apple trees.

Snow Drops

Sand edges the road, sticking to our shoes, sounding
Gritty as we press our feet against pavement;

The road curves now, leading down past the magnetic
Hill where we go sledding when the snow is soft—

Now green covers the round bulge of the land, like a
Topographical map with its indentations and ridges,

A hefty hill—before us, all winter turning over, some
Leftover red berries, a cluster of snow drops springing

Up in the underside of the moss, soft against the new
Growth of trees; across the way, the creek waters

Rush fast between the waves of newly sprouting grass.

Fallujah

i.

Place names pop up from across the globe—
Some of them we've heard before, some of them
New to us—marines lost, trucks jumped, dead
Bodies loaded into the back—one man maniacal
Says nothing will stop us; right is on our side—
He will entertain no other plans; I listen,
Appalled, at his course of action—

ii.

We celebrate Easter, the coming of spring amidst
The shouts of hate, cries grow loader, for revenge,
Justice, a ceasefire; meanwhile, politicians split
Hairs as to whether any one of us could have seen
This coming; hairs caught in a microscope;
It is easy to speculate—

iii.

In retrospect, how many of these dots might have
Lined up if any of us had been paying slight attention
To what matters; separate but related, I tell my
Children that each one of them is a miracle; this, I
Believe; each of them, so quickly, could have not
Landed here in a—

iv.

Moment's flash of blinding light, so many decisions
Must be made.

Easter Song, Requiem

You look down at your little girl, blonde in sunlight,
And you tell her she will soon learn, she will know
What she's doing, how you find your way—

A balloon slips out of her hand, sliding up to the sky;
She cries darkness within—you tell her it will return,
In not so very long—

Forty years later, I see my daughter before me,
Lying next to her puppy, reading in spring
Sunlight; silently, I wish she may escape, fly

Free, find her own way, follow through what matters
To her, with no thought to what may stand in her way—

Still, you try to me that I am wrong, that I can't sing
The song, tone deaf, I can't get the pitch right—

For the first time I dream in the night—
I know that these things are not right, there is

Another road to travel—all along it is where I have
Wanted to go; that much I now know.

Late Night Bedtime

It is late night bedtime—we stayed up longer
Than we should have, in these days outside routine—
I've hugged, kissed, and tucked you in—

Your chin just covered by a blue sheet pulled taught;
The light is low, one lamp shines in from the hallway—

Your room—books stacked on shelves, computer parts
Stashed in the corner—I do not know the names of
Any of them—your bear and baby pillow tossed on
The floor, still—

Each time I leave, you call me back with something
More—it's related, you'll see—"can you snuggle me?"

Each time, I've lain down beside you, your breaths
Fall even and deep, you're already close to sleep—

"Mommy, can moms die of breast cancer?"
"Sometimes," I say, "but not usually."
"Oh."

Your best friend's mom has just been diagnosed—
I see how your shore up your world, by method,
Rationality, and reason—

"One more kiss," I say, as I turn away, flicking the
Last light on my way, I see you are at last fast
Asleep.

The Toy Airplane

Blue sky spreads out before us—
Not a cloud on this April day, world
Has been waiting for sun—no leaves yet—
Simply branches bare, hence no
Shadows of leaves—low wind on an
Open day—hours spread out without
Plans, no homework, no practice—

A toy airplane to fly—it takes off, sours
Above, turns, curves towards an
Almost perfect landing—we take
What comes—just one more trip
You say—

Your face open, expectant, a final
Flight lands in the top branches of
An apple tree—first you climb, then
Me—on a rescue mission high
Above our waiting orchard.

Filaments

April filaments stretch across spring air—
Chill, foggy, and rainy—far too cold for this
Time of year—

Sudden bursts of heat from a brushfire burn
Out of control, surprising us that summer
Could come—

On a Sunday, I look skywards and wish for
Peace in my soul;

No one else but me can figure out where I
Want to be;

How this life came over me; doubt, I send
You away as words warm my mind.

Were There Deer in the Garden of Eden?

I wonder: were there deer in the garden of Eden?
Did they trample through the grass, picking up a
Stray apple from Eve's grasp? Were there deer in

The garden of Eden? Did they wander free and
Clear—did they wait for Eve to give the signal?
If life is spent attempting to conform to a

False idea, a fictional standard of perfection, then
How can we say we are not avenged as sinners?
If poetry is a form of prayer, how do we tell, as

Yeats asked, the dancer from the dance? As deer
Wander in twilight—how do we know they are
There if the mist is too thick to see through—

A mirage comes upon us; when did we decide
A woman was responsible for the seed of evil?

The Murder of a Small Child

I thought he was the devil so I strangled him—
Thus the story begins: a small boy, angry, tired,
Tousled challenges his mother, who is herself
Unstable, past any point of reason; in angry
Destruction for which she ever will punish
Herself and be penitent, repentant—so, she
Suffers immediately for what she cannot believe
She has done: taken the life of her own son,
Whether by madness or happenstance, or the
Terrible moods of fate—she held his neck so
Hard, fingers closed around his flesh, until his
Breathing ceased, quieted, stilled, suffocating.

Journey to the Spirit World: Red Lake Shootings

At best estimate, it takes three days to cross over into
Another world, where we know not what we may find—
Like the blind, we must put our trust in what we believe
To be true, so it is that the biggest mystery of our
Existence comes before us—

As if anew; we prepare for the journey, with blanket,
Water, and trophies, as though any of these material
Possessions could guide us, or make the slightest
Difference beyond the confines of what we believe is true.

Easter Monday

On this rainy day just past Easter, my parents' anniversary,
I think these thoughts—you, my daughter, how I love to say
Those words—may they always be true—I know I have to let
Go of you—

Otherwise, you cannot grow as I wish you to—how baffling
I find you, so like me in some respects, in others, so different—
Your upturned nose, your irrepressible giggle, your fevered
Determination to make a difference to our planet—

May you never lose your voice, or lower it in any way—
Because you are afraid what you say might not be true;
This much, and how much more, I pray for you—

April Fire

I toss a dried log on the starting wood—last fire, last of the year—
Already, we are beginning spring, or supposed to be, at least, as
We haltingly edge towards warmth; all this rainy Sunday afternoon
The flame burns until, at the final embers, I find one last piece of
Apple wood, forked, sawn from the midst of our orchard, a piece
Growing too high, gnawed by squirrels, perhaps a hungry deer—

Waiting for winter to end in this almost time; days lengthen after
Dawn; when we open the door, we can smell ashes, see last
Smoke rings curling, rising, winding from out the chimney.

New Month

This April light is thinned, ribbonned, twirling around us—no leaves
Yet on the trees, only the thinnest of buds beginning, satisfied—
Already we forget how soon snow is lost, still blocks of ice left
On our lawns—

We blink at newly bright sun casting shadows we're straining
To see, already, winter seems long past—we linger now in
Twilight, newly extended, daffodils shoot up, blooming on the
Other side of the stream where we walk, carelessly.

At the Gardner Museum, Spring

On this fragile, hot, bright April day, I do not want to bother
You with my ghosts—I have been here before, with my father,
Just a month ahead of the cancer diagnosis, which was already
Eating away at his mouth—

He wore a tie and jacket, already thinning around his slimming
Shoulders, clothes slipping past him—we laughed about how,
Just as I was gaining weight carrying twins, he was losing
Pounds, sliding off faster than he could account—the gazpacho
Soup tasted pretty good—

Went down better than he had hoped—my treat, we split a
Cannoli for dessert—after that, the tumor got to him, spreading
Its grasp down his throat until it strangled him;

You three—his grandchildren—are here now in this sunshine
Courtyard—you are his blessing—I do believe he knows that.

The Return

When you came back, the leaves were already falling into autumn—
You brought gifts: dolls, trinkets, marzipan—I didn't like the face of
The big porcelain doll; when I grabbed her too hard, I pulled off her
Long black hair in a clump. You reprimanded me—

The candy tasted strange, like cardboard; so you were not dead after
All, as I come to believe—

In the meantime, I had to begin all over again, except for the secret I
Never told you—all summer I had been practicing how to stop loving
You, rehearsing how to tell people you had died—

That I was now an orphan; that was a truth I never spoke aloud.

A Nature Walk, Oxbow

Go seek what you can—brown bark hanging off a shaggy hemlock
Tree, fiddle-head ferns springing up, uncurling from their winter
Tightness, uncoiling, rejoicing in new oxygen let in, miniature violets
In bloom, the color of deadly nightshade, beaver chips—

Leftover from some midnight snacking; it's a miracle no one
Falls into the creek that warming afternoon of possibility.

Goal, Spring Soccer

You run down the field, lanky and long now—your head held high,
Looking toward the sky—your feet deft, swift—you fake out the
Defense and with speed on your side, you shoot without flinching,
Or even hesitating for an instant—

The ball slides in and, when you see it's going to count, you break
Into your open-face, crooked tooth grin; you slap your teammates five
And, on your way back to line up, you slip me a sly smile—way to
Go, may you always be so bold.

Drumlin

Drumlin, dated from its first American usage in 1833, originally from the Irish,
Droimnin—our apple town is full of drumlins, places where glaciers moved
Across unformed till—a round word, full with sound, just right to describe
This mound of a magnetic hill, which rises and falls along a brush of trees,
A curving road lined with stone walls—

Toppling, undisturbed, in the middle of his pastoral landscape—after a rainy week,
Grass is electric green, lush, full, thick—this same hill was where we went
Sledding not so long ago—as seasons turn and fill—so we walk the hollows
And the ridges trying to find our way home.

Northern Leopard Frogs

We have done this walk through Oxbow in each season—in darkening
Autumn light, by tracks of snow is our shoes, and now on this uncommonly
Hot June day—each time, I see something new, something shown to me
By you—

Today, it is the frogs, green, speckled, and northern, as well as a toad or two,
Yellow star-cut flowers with fine petals, white lace weeds, a ladybug on the
Underside of a new leaf, a caterpillar stuck to a stick—new candle on
The pine trees—

The Pinus Rigida, browning pinecones decaying on the path, soft needles
Marking our trail, a freight train lumbering through the middle of a Sunday
Afternoon in almost summer—

Love Letters

Sultry June spreads over me in the afternoon following my
Father's death; at the instant his heart stopped, rains came and
Stayed until the noon we buried his ashes under the dogwood
Tree—

Its blossoms white stars, clusters of flowers edged by green springy
Leaves—

My mother hands me a packet of papers, brittle and yellowed—
Look at these for me, tell me what they are;

I take a peek, peeling back layers of dates until I recognize they
Are words penned in my father's spiky hand, letters professing
An intimacy certainly never meant for me to see—

The Transfer

I think of this day as both a beginning and an ending—
A departure and an arrival, a departure and a return;

Heavy with waiting, I drove to the Boston hospital so that
Our embryos could be returned to my body—

Giddy with valium and the news of how many eight cell
Beings had grown, I asked for five to be kept inside me—

The doctor joked we would soon be a large family—
The embryologist said our embryos were beautiful,

How lucky we were—afterwards, I rested and hoped—
Exactly one year later, I nursed the miraculous twins,
Born too soon—already five months old—

Before going to the cemetery on that June morning
To bury my father beneath the flowering Chinese
Dogwood tree.

The Reduction

I had to fight the urge to take August 13th as an omen, Friday the thirteenth—
It was a hot, lethargic morning—I drove to Boston early—

A statistic only bears meaning if it happens to you—

To save the two fetuses, I had to terminate the third;

The will for survival runs deep—

I could barely speak—

The procedure room was dark and quiet; my doctor did not have much to say—

After I told him I was ready to give this life away—a ghost child in the wind,
Forever lost against the current of what had to be.

Of course, nothing can exist without a state of risk.

The Transfusion

I can see them, I can see them—my mother repeats, as she weaves
Her way into my hospital room—

What's that? She asks, seeing the bag of blood attached to my arm—

I'm getting a transfusion, I lost a lot of blood at the birth—

Oh no, she croons—I demure—it's not a big deal, I will heal—

So, when can I see the babies, that's what I want to know—

Not right now, I declare; I'd like to be there when you first see them—

Can you please wait? I feel the stranger's blood dripping into my arm,
Suddenly warm at the mixing of other and mine—

The most dangerous thing a woman can do in America is give birth—
I don't remember whether she went to the nursery without me—

Over those important details, my mind is cloudy—we protect
Against that which we cannot bear to feel—my life has been
A series of unwindings, of allowing myself to feel again, so well
Did I learn to be numb?

Late Summer

As I slip into the ordinary, I am struck by the fact I will only
Be here a short while—

This summer, this pond, these children, will all slip away as
They may and that is how it should be—

I am only here as an afterthought, that is what happens—
We mothers become redundant, that is the routine, we all fight
It so—

What remains a mystery, long after you three have passed through
My body, that will be the end before the beginning—

The Seventh Day of the Seventh Month

On this inauspicious day, a sequence of bombs goes off across London,
Just as people are going to work; the timers release explosions into
The air, perfectly coordinated—

Leaving trains blown up far underground, the tops of buses soar and
Detach themselves from their bottoms in a hopeless chaos of
Destruction unleashed upon this brittle world;

Construction workers rush over to donate blood; doctors hurry to
The scenes, dots upon a map in black, mourning all these people
Caught in the tragic tangle of what we call terrorism.

Girl on Bus

A young girl who sits on a bus on her way to work is blown to pieces—
Nothing to be salvaged, nothing saved—she is one of the first from

The blast to be identified—her face is known—that face has been loved
By her family who wished her well off into this new life, to begin again—

Instead, men wearing backpacks chose to ride the same bus, detonating
Their goods out of the mistaken idea where, to do so, would transport

Them to an afterlife where a God would preside, a good God, their God.

On Not Being Sure of My Biological Father

I stare at this face looking back at me from the biography—
A handsome man with a long forehead, a strong nose, not

Unlike my own father—as I pore over every feature, I wonder
All over again whether he was the one who gave his sperm so

I could—I grab on to certain facts: he was a runner, a national
Track star, he had six heart attacks—was known to be a brilliant,

If problematic scientist, possessing a cutting-edge mind—but
Was he mine? Do my ice blue eyes match his, by the geometric

Principle of congruence, he looked like me, but does that one
Observation carry all the meaning we need to know?

Dawn Over Akron

Even the name of this city sounds harsh, acrid, as it pokes
Smokestacks towards brightening August sky, preparing to
Spool fire, ash, and detritus towards a few clouds—

A new day here, a Saturday, no rush to work, instead a
Few tenders of pokers remain in watch—ready for any
Sign of distress—

Few joys remaining, patients in hospitals awakening,
Wanting another day of living—the victims of a bombing
Hope for recovery and its possibilities—

A uniform dullness prevails as we cross the flyovers,
Hurtling towards the outskirts, a new ugliness between us.

The News

Can it wait? my father asks, throat clogged with mucus and phlegm,
Never to open entirely again—*No, not this time.*

Well, what is it, then? my father inquires through the receiver on
This frigid January morning—he is his hospital, me in mine—across
Boston—

You're a grandfather, twice over—

So soon? Yes, I say, *yes, the twins have made their way into this world—*
New lives begun, two hearts beating, two sets of lungs breathing—

Hanging on to life, groggy from delivery and blood loss, my body pulsing,
Reeling with excitement, adrenaline, the rush of giving birth not once,

But twice—*We named him after you, a boy and girl,* I think he grasps
What I am saying—there is a pause—

I vow to improve so that I can see them and you.

Five months later, he will die.

Cleaning House

I find my father's death certificate—once I knew every detail on
That form—a document which only told part of one story, just
Part—he died at 12:50, I thought it was 12:08 when the call came—

Already I've forgotten important details—

Slipped inside the cover a book, I find a notice for my mother's
Piano recital when she was fifteen, telling me she played
Beethoven on an afternoon when she was fifteen—

In a New York city apart; I find the miniature blue hat my son
Wore when he was born—I can still smell milk and him—

These belongings bring me back.

East Bare Hill Pond

All summer long, we've come to this pond, the four of us—
We've seen the blue heron swoop down, swoon his wings,
Flutter in awkwardness before he lands on lily pads—

Opening now with still yellow flowers—almost blue water,
Cottages ring the shore, reaching out to islands dotted on
Rocky spots scattered through the rippling wake—

Swim lessons, pick-up games of pickle, diving off second
Raft, waiting for the return trip of the ice cream truck to
Lick sweet strawberry coconut concoctions—the bell

Rings announcing its arrival, on our penultimate morning
Here, I smell ripening grapes on vines—it is no longer our time.

The Carousel (II)

The park is darkening now, light slipping—
Every ride and entertainment outlined in
Twinkling white bulbs, little children have

Departed for tubs and bed—older ones
Have just begun arriving for revelry—I
Hold your hand as light falls—

Like a fun house mirror, I see the world
Distorted—a man runs past me, his
Face contorted from burns and scars—

I see a lost child crying, searching for
Her parents everywhere—horses turn,
Music swoons, and I see all of these scenes

In front of me churning through life's stream.

Last August Orchard Days

At this close of August, I strain against the edge of uncertainty,
Darkness comes sooner now, days blur by and I know much
Less than I thought I might be now—

What I hold can fit in one palm—one ripe golden apple has
Fallen from our tree by the driveway, it drops into the
Sandy road leading to our house, for now—

We catch nettles' chokes, perhaps sidestepping the worst.

Hurricane Katrina

Some things pass degrees beyond human understanding—
Water has risen, levees have caved, bulging under the
Unexpected weight, debris rushing toward them until
There is no way to get out—the only way to go is up high—

By helicopters reaching into the sky—parents have been
Separated from their babies—the missing lost in rivers of
Water, rushing toward the sea, racing to find an opening—
To get across, people are told, don't look down, not

Under any circumstances—bodies are floating, both animal
And human; an entire underworld sea has been unearthed,
Shallow grave markers have pried up from soil, swirling

In pools of mud—nothing more than this remains to say.

Bradford Pear Trees, September 2005

Even the pear trees are confused—having lost their leaves, had them
Ripped off in high winds, they think it's spring—they've started
Blooming again, too early, or too late—

However you may see it, bursts of soft white blossoms have sprung
On their branches, perhaps pears will come before winter, before
Anyone is ready—

Least of all the trees—the rest have stood in high water, with their
Roots soaked—no one knows how long they will live—this territory
Is all new, unfamiliar, as we struggle to settle, to stop

The flood, to sweep away the debris, we see how futile those searches
May be—as we come to rest where once made a beginning—

As each human being must learn to do.

New Orleans, Two Months Out

Still how can there be almost 4,000 people missing from when
The waters rose, the levees broke, and the town drowned in its
Own vile sludge—

Turning everything it touched brown, darkening whatever had
Been white, making it, at best, barely salvageable—nothing is
Left to be rebuilt—

The city wails for a leader, for a good turn, for someone to say,
Here, this is what we can do together—

In a vacant schoolyard, kids play pick-up dodgeball instead of
Going to class; here there are no teachers, no books, only a

Ghost town almost lost—

Let's consider what can be saved.

The Old Shirley Meeting House

A spare white meeting house sits square on a green lawn,
Clearing swept, a common ground to make space for
Light, and soul—

Air is musty, still close from summer's heat, apples' new
Scent—a stray fly buzzing yet, zinging up and down along
The pews—

You, my youngest son, walk up to play your piece on
This grand piano, lid open—as you begin your fingers find
The notes—

My mind wanders to a day now four years away when
You and I waited at the train station for your father on
September 11th—

That was a close one—your concentration breaks, tears
Almost come—later, belatedly, I hug you when
No one else is looking.

On the Not So Invisible War

Five soldiers from a Scranton battalion are lost, missing, assumed dead—
Can't listen to the news anymore, she says, there's no good news to hear—
When the word is bad, I'm sure I'll learn it faster than I need to know—

Can barely stand the sound in my ear—my son has already been to Iraq
And back twice, that's more than I can ask for in terms of grace—I see her
Face, she only wants her child back safe, that's all—

But this is the new way of war—when they write the history of this mess,
We will know they've got it all backwards, upside down.

White Giraffe

What would it be like to be a white animal in the desert, unable to hide away
From prey and predator alike—

Caught in the sleek light from the sun, with nowhere to run, all on your own—
With nowhere to seek camouflage, or subterfuge, simply have broken

All the rules, feeling like a fool for being the only one left during a drought,
With the water basin empty, unable to see her reflection in the slowly draining

Supply of what might simply mean a place to begin, a place where we might
Begin to know ourselves—

Oh white giraffe, show us your showy, unsteady ways.

October Moon

Full blue sky stretches high above us, already clear with morning light—
A few leaves scattering down to the ground beside us—

We look up and see a round orb, an omen, the moon fuller than ever
Before, sketched and stretched with the opaque of white, of clarity,

Now speckles, of the knowledge that you now learn and pull within you—
That the glowing moon is there all the time, it's just that some of the time

We cannot see it—you learn so much now, every day—I pray that you may
Take what there is good from this world—and pull it inside you—that we will

Know this place as if for the first time.

Barn Clearing

In late afternoon November, I haul and pick my way through
A decade worth of leavings—a wheelbarrow, a child's broken
Tree swing, a rocking horse, two bookcases, mouse pilings—

Nests enmeshed in an old blue coverlet, one a spread for a
Marital bed—tractor parts, screws, half a rake, an apple tree
Ladder leaning up against surplus cedar boards; once, a horse

Boarded here, at least one, maybe two in stalls—once
Mucked out and cared for—my daughter always begged for
Horses—now just a feed bag left half open

On the dirt floor—we are only passing through here—I who
Thought I was making my life here—I was, apparently, deceived.

Letter to the World (after Emily Dickinson)

If no one ever reds these words, pronounces these sounds, but
Passes over the, these vowels and consonants of my heart—
Does it matter?

Does it then mean they do not exist?

Do they not matter if they have not made their way into the
World—my replacement for the eighty plus notebooks
That got tossed in the dump—

Note, my use of the passive voice—no, it was not my idea to
Take my old journals to the dump, it was not indeed, but
Then again,

I did not say no when presented with the request—these
May flutter and pit their way into the world, but then again,
If they stay in the closet, then no one will ever know—

I think of them as my letter to the universe, the only way I
Know how to say that which I can, to elucidate my grief,
My joy, my misery, my ecstasy—all that is secret in me—

All that is human, in spirit or otherwise, I think of you, my
Father, as you bade me prop open your hospital door so

That it let just enough light in, on your thin coverlet—
The light over the Charles—Boston, sunset—

I think you knew you were leaving then—did you know
All that was in me?

The White Pine Tree

Ten years ago, I watched a harvest moon rise up from below our hill—
Burnt orange, close to tangerine it would seem—bulging, bulbous,
Hanging as though it might have fallen out of the sky had it tried—

That was at the end of October, close to Halloween—and, since, I've
Measured time and seasons by dusky moonrise—

A few days before I write this, my eldest son showed me a flock of black
Birds cackling loudly, in rushed descent to landing atop the pine—

A stopping place, he reminded me—we'd seen them there last year,
Just this time—the branches shook when they all departed,

All at once, for points southwards.

Skidding

For hours now, we've been driving through rough terrain; mountain
Passes begin and end, then begin again—

Clouds closing in on us, slowly—our vision obfuscates until I can only
See through a tiny patch of windshield, cross winds begin to tangle
Our way, to bump us around;

We pass a streak of accidents—two fire engines, a rolled over car,
Dazed people wandering in the chill—a man walking a black dog on a hill

Staying away from the rescue workers who are unfolding stretchers—
Others racing to seek help;

I press my foot too hard on the accelerator—my eldest son, sitting beside
Me, and I go into a spin—

He knows to press traction control; when we turn right way round, I'm shaking.

Heather Corbally Bryant is a Lecturer in the Writing Program at Wellesley College; previously she taught at Penn State University and Harvard College where she won awards for her teaching. She received her AB from Harvard and her PhD from the University of Michigan. Her first book, *How Will the Heart Endure: Elizabeth Bowen and the Landscape of War* (University of Michigan Press) won the Donald Murphy prize from the ACIS. She has published poems in *The Christian Science Monitor, Sixteen, Fourth & Sycamore, The Paddock Review, Old Frog Pond Farm Chapbooks* and in the anthologies: *In Another Voice* and *Open-Eyed, Full-Throated: An Anthology of American/Irish Poetry* (Dublin: Arlen House, 2019) *Cheap Grace,* her first chapbook was published by Finishing Line Press. Her second collection of poems, *Lottery Ticket,* was published in 2013 by the Parallel Press Series of the University of Wisconsin Libraries-Madison. Her third chapbook, *Compass Rose*, appeared in 2015 from Finishing Line Press. *My Wedding Dress,* her first long collection of poems, was published by Finishing Line Press in 2016. *Thunderstorm,* her second full-length volume of poetry, was published by Finishing Line Press in the fall of 2017. It was nominated for a Mass Book Award in 2018. Her sixth collection of poetry, *Eve's Lament,* was published by Finishing Line Press in the winter of 2018. Her seventh collection of poetry, *James Joyce's Water Closet,* (2018) won honorable mention in the Open Chapbook Competition of Finishing Line Press. Two of her poems were nominated for a Pushcart Prize in 2018. Her eighth collection of poetry, *Leaving Santorini,* appeared in 2018. *Practicing Yoga in a Former Shoe Factory*, her ninth collection of poems (and her fourth full-length one) was published in the spring of 2020. She has given readings across the United States, and in Ireland.

www.ingramcontent.com/pod-product-compliance
Lightning Source LLC
Chambersburg PA
CBHW021149090426
42740CB00008B/1011